Billie Jean King's
Secrets of Winning Tennis

Billie Jean King's
Secrets of Winning Tennis
Billie Jean King and Joe Hyams

Holt, Rinehart and Winston
New York Chicago San Francisco

Published simultaneously in Canada by Holt, Rinehart
and Winston of Canada, Limited

Library of Congress Cataloging in Publication Data
King, Billie Jean.
Billie Jean King's secrets of winning tennis.
1. Tennis—Miscellanea. I. Hyams, Joseph, joint
author. II. Title. III. Secrets of winning tennis.
GV995.K49   796.34'22   74-5095
ISBN 0-03-013141-3

Photographs by John Hamilton, Globe Photos, Inc.

Published, November, 1974
Second Printing, January, 1975

Printed in the United States of America

CONTENTS

v

Contents

INTRODUCTION

Many people think that because I am an athlete and like to compete I must be tough. To my surprise this attitude even exists among some of the so-called women's libbers. It just seems to be a generally accepted fact that a woman who is competitive in her career must also be competitive in her personal life.

I don't agree with this notion at all (and neither does my husband). Although I play tennis competitively to win, I don't like to beat men. I've beaten them in practice and they were crestfallen. I beat Bobby Riggs and felt badly about it because the match was publicized as a battle between the sexes. It wasn't that at all. It was a competition between a young athlete and an aging athlete and, despite the male chauvinists, the outcome was predictable. I am younger and, at this stage of our careers, Bobby's and mine, I am the better player, and that's all there is to it.

It is still true, nevertheless, that a good man can beat a good woman if they are more or less of equal age. There's no way I could beat Rod Laver, Stan Smith, or Pancho Gonzales. But I think at some time in the future we may very well have a woman win the world championship of tennis.

The woman champion of the future will probably be one who has been brought up differently than most of today's women. She will not have to face discrimination in sports and will probably be a woman who has been a good all-around athlete since childhood, accustomed to competing against men without any mental hangups.

That was not my case. I was brought up to be a wife, to consider men physically superior, and to look at sports strictly as a man's occupation. When I was in junior high school and turned down invitations to slumber parties at girls' homes in favor of tennis tournaments, my friends thought I was an oddball.

I soon learned it was not a good idea to beat a boy I liked. It's amazing how losing to a girl can turn a guy off. Most fellows consider the girl who is a better athlete a threat. The only men who don't think this way are, in my view, the real men; these are the men who have their own thing, too, and no one can take that away from them.

But I loved tennis and as the daughter of parents with a low income (my father was a Long Beach fireman), I felt that if I could become proficient at tennis maybe I could travel and meet people — a notion the other girls laughed at.

I persisted, however, and learned that if a woman wants to make sports a career she has to be strong-willed because most everyone will try to discourage her. Even today it's a tough psychological battle for the girl who wants to be an athlete but I think it's getting easier thanks to the increasing number of women athletes who are successful and popular.

Many people still think that a woman can't be competitive because she can't stand up to the emotional pressure. I think, however, that anyone who saw my match against Bobby Riggs realized that I was under intense emotional pressure, not because I was a woman, but because I was an athlete in an all-out endeavor against another athlete.

Tennis is my thing and I love it. The aesthetics of the game turn me on. There are few thrills in life for me that compare with hitting a particular shot just right at a given moment — knowing that my balance is perfect, that the ball has hit the pocket of the racket, and that it has taken me fifteen years of steady practice and playing to make the right shot at the right time.

But, first, you have to have a natural talent to develop. Then, when you have developed that talent to the utmost of your personal capabilities and you hit that one almost perfect shot, the payoff is a tingling feeling deep inside and all through your body that must be comparable to that of the musician who thinks he has discovered the lost chord.

That's why, for me, tennis is such a fascinating and creative sport. There's a constant challenge in making the ball do exactly what you want it to do and there are constant decisions: shall I use a spin or a slice, shall I lob or go down the line or hit cross-court? All the choices are there, laid out for the player just as the colors are laid out on a palette for the artist. And the frustrations are there, too.

I don't think anyone has ever hit the absolutely perfect shot any more than anyone has ever painted the perfect picture or written the perfect sentence. Most creative things in life can be improved, so I keep on practicing and practicing. Practice is the name of the game.

There are no shortcuts to playing tennis. There's only practice and more practice and experience. In this book I have tried to distill the knowledge of nineteen years of active tennis playing and constant experimentation, always searching for new ways to improve on old techniques.

The section on serving, for example, reflects the results of some of this experimenting. The serve should be the easiest shot to learn in tennis because it's the only stroke in which the player has complete control over how he makes contact with the ball. Despite this, the serve seems to be difficult for most players to learn.

This set me to thinking that perhaps the fault lay with the instruction, not the student.

After much trial and error, my associates at my Tennis America schools and I evolved a method of teaching the serve which, I feel, is relatively easy for the student and very effective. This book presents the method in print for the first time.

Although this book is at times female oriented, the truth is there's very little difference between the types of game played by men and women. Good tennis is good tennis, and a tennis ball doesn't know whether it was hit by a man or a woman.

So, read on. Then go out and practice and play. Maybe you will discover the thrill that has thus far eluded me – the thrill of making the perfect shot and playing the perfect game.

Billie Jean King

Billie Jean King's
Secrets of Winning Tennis

1.
LESSONS
AND
LEARNING

What is the best age to start learning how to play tennis?

I had never heard of tennis before I was eleven years old and took my first lesson, but today more and more youngsters are becoming aware of tennis at an early age. However, I think a child under eight or nine is too young to absorb the fundamentals of the game and will probably find it dull and the racket heavy.

Conversely, I don't think any age is too old to start learning. It's amazing how tennis can open up a whole new life for any person and help him feel healthier, whatever his age. And if people make the least bit of progress you can't believe how happy they become.

There's another side effect for older people who start learning how to play: they start meeting other people.

In this day and age, when we have so much leisure time and many of us are overweight, playing tennis is a good way to exercise, keep fit, and have fun whether you start at fifty and play until you're eighty or whether you start when you're ten.

How do you suggest a youngster prepare for tennis?

The main thing for a youngster is to learn all kinds of sports when young. The reason most girls and many boys can't serve is that they have never learned how to throw a ball properly. Instead of throwing with their elbow high behind their head, they throw from the hip. Any sport in which a youngster must throw a ball and must run is good preparation for tennis. That hand and eye coordination is important in tennis.

Is tennis a difficult game to learn?

Tennis is no harder to learn than any other game, but it may be especially difficult for women who didn't throw a ball in their childhood. The resulting lack of development in hand and eye coordination is an obstacle to overcome.

Unless you happen to be extremely gifted, there is no such thing as instant gratification in tennis. To hit a small moving object while you are moving takes a fair amount of coordination; it takes even more to hit a ball over a net 36 inches high, at its lowest point, into a singles court 39 feet long and 27 feet wide.

How long should it take the average person to learn to play?

That depends on his natural ability and how much he practices. I know people who will have a pro give them a playing lesson once or twice a week but these people never play against anyone except the pro who, let's face it, can make even a miserable player look good. They have been deluded into thinking they play good tennis, while the truth is they will never improve but will stay at the same level unless they get out in competition.

The average person should be able to play with

people at his level almost immediately, and the more he practices the better he will play.

Should a woman's course of instruction differ from a man's?

No. The fundamentals are the same for men and women.

Does it help or hurt to be a lefty?

Since most players are right-handed, it's usually an advantage to be a lefty. Your serve will have a natural slice into the backhand in the ad court and away from the forehand in the deuce court. Most of your other shots also will spin in the opposite direction of a right-hander, which means the majority of your opponents will have to reverse their normal strategy.

How should I choose a teacher?

Find a person whom you feel really knows tennis and rely primarily on that person's advice. At the same time be receptive to new ideas. Until you become aware of your own strengths and weaknesses, you won't have a frame of reference with which to figure out why you want to do certain things.

What do you think of group lessons?

I had my first free lessons when I was eleven, courtesy of the Long Beach Recreation and Park Commission, and I didn't have a private lesson until I was seventeen. I learned the basics of tennis in the public parks and I think I benefited immensely because in that kind of situation you learn from others and you teach them as they teach you. Everyone progresses at about the same speed and you always have someone of your ability or even better as your opponent.

Tennis camps are good for the same reason although they are expensive. However, at a camp such as any of the fourteen run by Tennis America, a student who hits the ball six hours a day should improve even without instruction. Students are given a foundation which lasts them a lifetime and once they leave camp they can teach themselves or reeducate themselves, which is the goal of all teaching.

When I go to camp, which is at least once a year, I think over and over about the basics and fundamentals. I know that even the best players in the world go back to the basics from time to time and take lessons to sharpen strokes that may have fallen off or to rid themselves of bad habits.

Is it possible to learn from watching matches on television?

Indeed it is. One can learn a lot from watching any level of tennis. You can learn a lot about strategy and stroke production from watching the pros and can frequently spot your own failings when watching players at your own or lower levels.

When I was a youngster I used to watch Pancho Gonzales and Lew Hoad play in Los Angeles, and watching them made me play better and inspired me to keep trying. Even if you're not aware of the finer points of professional play, some of it has to come across to you, and the more you watch, the more information you will pick up.

How long do you think a private lesson should last?

I think it's better to have two half-hour lessons each week than one 1-hour lesson because your concentration span will cover more of the lesson. In the beginning there's a lot to learn, and something new always takes time to sink in. One half-hour of having someone explain tennis is enough for most people at the start.

What are the most important strokes to learn?

The most important strokes for anyone, male or female, are the ground strokes.

Which should be learned first: the forehand or the backhand?

The forehand and backhand should be taught, learned, and practiced together.

It's ridiculous for a player to take two or three extra steps just to avoid his backhand when that shot is as easy to learn as the forehand and in many respects easier.

What usually happens is that the beginner first learns the forehand drive and, having reached the point where he can hit that shot fairly well, he avoids the backhand out of fear or distrust. Don't make that mistake. I am not dogmatic about many things but I am about this.

5

If you spend a half-hour on your forehand, spend a half-hour on your backhand and never, never run around either shot.

Is there one correct way to play tennis?

The fundamentals are the same for all the top players regardless of their style. Whenever you watch a tennis match you'll notice that very few players have the same overall approach to the game, whatever their level. Some players like the big serve-and-volley game as I do, while others like to stay on the baseline and hit ground strokes. Some find a happy middle ground between the two extremes. Chris Evert hits a two-handed backhand. Beverly Baker Fleitz doesn't hit a backhand. She is totally ambidextrous and hits a right-handed and left-handed forehand. Françoise Durr has a wristy backhand but good accuracy. Margaret Court uses her height and reach to overwhelm her opponents.

Everyone has his own style. Whenever I lose a match, someone tries to tell me what I did wrong. Although I may listen to him I have to filter out what I don't think is relevant and consider only the advice that sounds right for my game.

Do you recommend that a beginner learn a two-handed stroke?

No, unless you haven't enough strength to hit the ball with one hand.

I know that today a two-handed stroke is somewhat in vogue because of some of the young players who use it, like Cliff Drysdale, Jimmy Connors, and Chris Evert. As a result, other young players are trying to emulate them. But there is no clear advantage to a two-handed stroke for the average player.

Most people who use a two-handed stroke started playing that way as youngsters when they were not strong enough to hold the racket with one hand. As they developed, they liked the feeling of holding the racket with two hands and their perception of the ball was related to how they had started playing, so they continued that way.

But a two-handed stroke requires faster footwork and better timing than a one-handed stroke and a two-handed stroke limits the variety of shots you can hit. We don't teach two-handed strokes at my Tennis America schools.

Should I take lessons to change my strokes?

If you want to improve it's almost imperative that you take lessons.

When I was twenty-one, I was the fourth-ranked women's player in the world, with aspirations of becoming Number One. I knew I couldn't do it unless I changed my game radically. So I went to Australia for a year and took lessons from Mervyn Rose, who had been a pro and is considered one of the best coaches in the world.

That year was one of the most difficult — and gratifying — of my life because I changed my game drastically from a forehand to a serve game. And I learned how to play percentage tennis.

I still recall playing a match where I had thirty-five double faults with my new serve because I couldn't get the rhythm of it. But I stuck with the serve and within a year I was Number One.

A lot of people don't realize that even the pros take

lessons constantly, often from one another. Rod Laver, Ken Rosewall, and Pancho Gonzales helped me from time to time just as I have occasionally helped them.

The thing to remember is that if you take lessons to change your strokes, your game may get worse for a while but in the long run it will probably improve. You just have to stick to it, and if you have difficulties, remember me and my thirty-five double faults.

Is there an Australian way of playing?

Yes. You'll notice that players from different countries tend to have different styles and approaches. Australians, for example, are taught a lot of top spin, and now American coaches are teaching it to their players.

Do you suggest a beginner play with a heavy ball or a light one?

I think beginners benefit from learning with a heavy ball because then you have to learn to hit through the ball in order to carry it any distance. Australians play with a heavy ball, and the first year I played down there I had difficulty getting the ball to the service line from the backcourt. But I learned to hit through the ball during that year and my game improved.

Do you recommend jogging as an exercise for tennis?

It certainly helps a beginner get into shape before playing, and it's a good leg strengthener. I suggest that anyone who is out of shape consult his doctor first and then perhaps start jogging a quarter of a mile and work slowly up to a mile.

Is there such a thing as the perfect tennis player?

No. I've won a lot of tournaments and I can honestly say that even now I'm not entirely satisfied with the way I play. No matter how good you eventually become you will always know that there is a way to play just a little bit better.

When should I consider changing teachers?

After you have taken a few lessons seek some advice from other sources, either from books or from good players you know personally. Then you will have a good cross section of opinion from which to choose.

2.
THE
RACKET

Should a child learn with a small or a standard racket?

Small, child-size rackets are great for kids, especially in the beginning when they can't handle the weight of a heavier racket.

Is an expensive racket an advantage at the start?

You don't have to start to take lessons with the most expensive racket. First see if you like the game and if you want to get involved with it. Then graduate into a more expensive racket if you think your game warrants it.

Do you recommend learning with a metal or wood racket?

Generally speaking, when people learn with a metal racket they never learn to hit the ball properly. They let the racket do all the work and they start to slap at the ball. They never learn the concept of carrying the ball on the face of the racket for a long period of time, which I consider one of the most important concepts to learn early.

I don't think anyone should use a metal racket until he or she is quite proficient or is playing all the time.

The Racket

A metal racket has a tendency to give the ball a trampoline effect that makes it more difficult to control. On a metal racket all the strings do equal work, whereas on a wood racket only the short cross strings do the actual work, therefore you must put more effort into hitting a ball with a wood racket. As a result, your follow-through is better with wood, as is your stroking concept.

Should I start with a light or heavy racket?

My feeling is that you should start with the racket weight you will most likely be using for play. I strongly recommend a light racket for almost everyone. My own racket is 13 to 13¼ ounces strung. The weight of the racket has nothing to do with the player's strength. For example, Rod Laver, Cliff Richey, and Pancho Gonzales use the same weight as I do, and, being men, they are certainly stronger than I am. Most women should probably use 12½- to 13-ounce rackets, at the most 13½ ounces.

For reasons that elude me, many people seem to think that they get more power from a heavy racket, not realizing that power and pace are generated by the momentum of the head of the racket when it makes contact with the ball and by the length of time the ball and racket are in contact. The lighter the racket the quicker you are likely to get it around to meet the ball.

Should the racket be light or heavy in the head?

That's a matter of personal preference. I prefer it light in the head with the weight nearer the throat because I like to get the racket head around quickly and

11

I use a lot of wrist when I play. The farther away its weight, the more difficult it is to control. The only way to determine your own preference, however, is to experiment with various rackets and see which one feels most natural when you swing it.

Is it better to use a rectangular or a hexagonal handle?

I use a rectangular shape because I learned to play by holding the racket in a Continental grip. People who learn to play by holding the racket in an Eastern grip generally prefer a hexagonal shape.

How do I determine the proper circumference of the racket handle?

The majority of rackets sold today are 4½ inches. So when you go to a store to select a racket pick up a 4½ light and shake hands with it. See how your thumb lines up with the first knuckle of your second finger. If your thumb meets the point of the knuckle, the handle is probably correct. If the thumb extends beyond the knuckle, the handle is probably too small, and if the thumb falls short of the knuckle, the handle is probably too large. You might also have someone try to twist the head of the racket while you are holding it in the forehand grip. It should not turn too easily.

Should my racket be strung with nylon or gut?

That depends on how much money you can pay for a string job and how much you plan to play. If you are going to play often you will probably be better off with gut, which is more sensitive and responsive than nylon. Otherwise, nylon is cheaper and requires less care.

Although all professional players use gut, I doubt that anyone but a pro can tell the difference between gut and nylon if the racket is properly strung.

How tightly should I have my racket strung?

I don't feel a beginner should have a racket strung too tightly because you want to keep the ball on the racket strings as long as possible, since that's how you get the best control. My own rackets are strung medium to medium-tight.

3.
FEMALE
QUESTIONS

Do you think it is all right to play tennis during menstruation?

Since that's a normal situation for most women, I see no reason why they shouldn't play unless a doctor advises against it. As a pro I must play, whatever my physical condition, and I have found that menstruation doesn't affect me.

Do you suggest that a person who wears glasses switch to contact lenses when playing?

I find contact lenses uncomfortable but many players, including Arthur Ashe, tell me they prefer soft contacts because they don't have blind spots and it is easier for them to get accustomed to the change in perception.

I usually wear granny-type glasses on the court because the small, flat surface seems to have less distortion than the aviator or larger-type glasses.

Does the fact that most women are shorter than men affect their game?

I am only 5 feet 4½ inches tall, which makes me one of the shortest champions in pro tennis, and I find there are advantages and disadvantages to being short.

Usually a shorter person like myself is quicker off the mark and has quicker hands than someone taller. But if you're short and you find an opening you usually have to go for it in a big way. And when you're serving you must hit up and out more often than a taller person has to. I have always tried to make up for my lack of height by my shot production, speed, and accuracy.

Must a woman be a good athlete to play tennis?

In my view mental attitude is almost as important as athletic ability. But anyone who wants to play tennis well must be in good physical condition.

What is the most important stroke for a woman to learn?

The most important strokes for anyone, male or female, are the ground strokes.

How long into her pregnancy should a woman play?

I know women who kept on playing tennis until they went to the hospital. If a woman is accustomed to playing a lot of tennis, it might help her to keep her weight down during pregnancy if she continued to play. In any event this is an individual matter and the final decision should be up to a doctor.

Do you protect yourself against the sun?

The sun can be hard on skin and age it. For that reason most women would be well advised to put suntan lotion on their face, arms, and legs on bright days. And I feel they would be wise to wear a sun hat or visor. I've tried hats from time to time but I can't hack it. I always feel there's a roof over my head.

Do you feel a woman should wear a brassiere when she plays?

I wear one and so do most of the women on the pro circuit, even those women who don't wear bras off the court. I'm so small in front it really doesn't make any difference one way or the other, but I do think it's important for a woman to wear a bra, especially if she has a substantial bust.

Is playing tennis a good way to lose weight?

Not for me it isn't, but then I'm in condition. Someone who is out of condition would probably benefit from the exercise and movement.

I also feel that if a woman starts playing tennis and keeps the eating habits she had before, she's bound to lose weight. She has to be careful that she doesn't start increasing her eating and drinking, especially her consumption of soft drinks. I try to stay away from sweet liquids when I play and just sip a little water from time to time.

Do you suggest vitamin pills?

I take vitamins, including about 400 units a day of Vitamin E, because it increases my circulation and helps me avoid leg cramps. Margaret Court had a problem with leg cramps and found she could avoid them by taking potassium tablets, so I've added these tablets to my daily diet. I also take salt pills during the week before a match, especially if I am going to play in hot weather.

Do you think tennis is good for older women?

One of the nicest things about tennis is you can play at any speed you want. I know of many older women who play a very nice, sedate, and leisurely type of game and get a lot of fun out of it.

Do you think women must wear white on the court?

I don't feel it's important how a person dresses for tennis. When I started playing tennis I wore cut-off jeans or whatever I had. Too many people are inhibited about starting the game because of the cost of tennis clothes, even though it's possible today to buy outfits that are inexpensive. My feeling is that once someone really gets interested in tennis, she will realize that tennis clothes are designed with the sport in mind and are comfortable to play in as well as attractive and stylish.

How do you choose the proper clothes for playing?

The most important thing to me is comfort. No matter how attractive my outfit, if I'm uncomfortable or restricted in my movements I won't be able to hit the ball freely and move about quickly.

Do you smoke or drink?

I have an occasional beer when I'm not in training, but I've never smoked cigarettes. I tried pot once or twice but because I'm not accustomed to inhaling, my throat hurt and I was fuzzy headed the next day when I went out on the court. I think that anyone who wants to be a champion and is serious about athletics should refrain from taking any stimulant that would affect his coordination, stamina, and ability.

How do you handle tension?

I don't handle it; I use it. Generally I play best under pressure; that's what turns me on and that's what it's all about. Sometimes, if I think about a future match, I may get nervous, but then I tell myself, If you're a champion you've got to have guts. And when I get uptight or tentative on the court, I force myself to concentrate even more, and somehow I manage to get through it. It's a great feeling when you're able to beat your own fears as well as your opponent.

4.
GROUND
STROKES—
FOREHAND

What is the correct grip for a forehand?

The most important thing in tennis is understanding the relation of the face of the racket to the ball. During a match the average player might use any of a dozen variations in his grip. But basically there are two grips I recommend.

THE EASTERN GRIP is the grip most often used today by top players. To achieve it, hold the racket in your left hand, perpendicular to the ground; put your right hand flush against the strings and then slowly bring your hand to the racket handle and grasp it. When your fingers are spread comfortably, the V formed by your thumb and index finger should be directly on top of the racket handle.

THE CONTINENTAL GRIP is used by most Australians. It involves turning the racket another eighth of a turn to the right from the Eastern grip, so that the V now runs down the upper left corner of the handle. This is a very difficult grip for a beginner to be comfortable with and it requires more wrist control.

What grip do you prefer?

I favor a grip about halfway between a classic Eastern and a classic Continental, but I strongly recommend that most beginners start with the Eastern grip

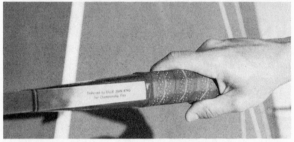

THE CONTINENTAL GRIP — Used mostly for
serving, it differs from the basic Eastern grip
only in that the racket is turned one-eighth to
the right.

and stay with it until they have a fairly steady forehand. Then you can experiment a bit until you find a grip that feels most comfortable to you.

Regardless of the grip you use, however, there is no time when the racket should be choked with a viselike or club grip. The racket should be held firmly enough so that it becomes a solid extension of your arm and it won't be jarred loose when you hit the ball, but at the same time the five fingers should be spread loosely around the handle so you can feel the racket through them.

What is the proper preparation for a forehand stroke?

The four main components of your preparation are the same for both forehand and backhand. They are:

1. Ready your position, keeping your eye on the flight of the ball.
2. Turn or pivot using the left hand to help draw the racket back.
3. Step toward the net.
4. Follow through, from low to high.

As the ball leaves your opponent's racket you should be in the ready position with your racket at waist level. When you see the ball coming to your forehand you should turn your body so that your left shoulder is pointing in the general direction of the flight of the ball. Your weight should be on your right foot.

After you have made the turn to your right, your feet should be planted in such a way that a line starting with your left foot, continuing through your right foot, and ending at the baseline will form a 45-degree angle with the baseline. You will then be in what is known as an open stance with the racket about even with your belt buckle.

Now, extend your arm as though you are reaching for something to the right of and slightly behind your right foot. Many players add a slight loop to this part of the swing to aid their rhythm and timing. A loop is all right so long as it's not exaggerated. In my view a linear or straight swing is preferable because it is quicker.

At the maximum point of your backswing the racket should be at no more than right angles to the net. If you take the racket back farther than that you won't be able to swing at the ball but will only be able to slap at it.

You should plan to make contact with the ball just even with your forward foot.

As you start the forward part of your swing keep your wrist firm, your arm steady, your head down, and your eyes on the ball right up to and beyond the moment of contact. The head of your racket should be even with your wrist or a little bit ahead of it. At the moment of contact your arm should be nearly fully extended.

Under no circumstances should you let the ball crowd in close to your body. This is a chronic problem for many players, even those at the advanced level, because it's natural to feel more secure if you hit the ball when it's close to the body.

When the ball bounces you should step and then— and only then—should you swing. Do not step and swing at the same time—the step has to first give you the base or stability to control your stroke. Your racket swing is from low to high and you should make direct contact with the ball off your front foot. You should finish the swing with the racket head at least at eye level.

What is the best way to bring back the racket?

Let's return to the basic geometry we've discussed from time to time. A straight line is the shortest distance between two points. The best way to bring back the racket is to do it quickly. The quickest way is obviously the shortest.

The player who today is the best example of economy of movement is Ken Rosewall. There is no wasted motion in any of his shots. Everything he does is directly related to hitting the ball; if it isn't he simply doesn't do it.

There is another advantage to simplicity: the more economical and simple your stroke the less effort you expend and the less tired you will become, which is an important factor when you are in a long match.

What are the types of forehand shots?

There are four types of forehand shots:

THE FLAT DRIVE is the basic forehand. The racket face is perpendicular to the ground at the moment of impact and the ball carries over the net with a minimum of spin.

THE CHOP is nothing more than an exaggerated slice. Take a high backswing, a short fast downward swing in which the racket is laid back at a 45-degree angle, and a low follow-through.

SIDE SPIN is most effective as a down-the-line approach shot. To execute it, you exaggerate the open stance and lay back the racket so that at the moment of impact your wrist is definitely in front of the racket head (thus violating one of the cardinal rules of the forehand). Keep the racket nearly parallel to the net during the follow-through. Properly hit, the ball will

THE FOREHAND — Ready
position, pivot and mid-
point of backswing,
stepping forward with left
foot (at moment of bounce)
and completion of
backswing, and four stages
of forward swing

stay low to the ground and when it bounces it will squirt off to your opponent's left. Many players, however, have a tendency to lay back the wrist so much that all power is gone from the shot.

THE TOP-SPIN drive is hit with overspin. You should drop the racket head just slightly during the backswing. Then, on making contact with the ball during the early part of the forward swing, roll the racket head over the top of the ball and complete your follow-through slightly higher than usual. This stroke gives a distinct top spin to the ball and its trajectory will be more rounded than that of a flat drive.

How can I aim the ball?

I dislike use of the word "aim" because many people become tentative when they think of aiming something.

If you make proper contact with the ball you direct it to where you want it to go by hitting through it.

Think of it this way: when you hit the ball with a low to high swing, catching it in the pocket of the racket, the ball will, at the moment of impact, actually compress and sink into the racket strings which encircle it, much as a trampoline does when a body falls into it. The ball will stay on the racket strings for about 6 to 10 inches of the swing and then catapult out.

During this brief but all-important moment of contact you can direct the ball anyplace you want it to go by keeping the ball on the strings, continuing to push out against the ball until the moment when the racket face is pointing exactly where you want the ball to go. The racket does not stop here, because you should hit through the ball by letting the racket continue into what is called the follow-through, but your exertion should stop at this point.

How can I hit a "heavy ball"?

It's difficult to know what causes a heavy ball because certain players hit such a ball and others don't. I know it has nothing to do with the speed — two people can hit the ball with the same speed but one ball will be heavy and the other ball light. I assume that the person who hits the heavier ball keeps it on the racket strings a fraction of a second longer.

How should I hit a forehand cross-court?

Hit the ball 6 inches in front of your left leg. To hit down the line you hit it 6 inches behind your left leg. At the same time the racket is laid back ever so slightly so that your wrist is just a little bit in front of your racket head at the moment of impact. In a cross-court, the racket head is just a bit ahead of your wrist.

How high should the follow-through be?

Your follow-through is the right height if, when it's finished, you can see over your arm, without the whole arm being visible when looking straight ahead. If you can see under your arm your follow-through is too high, and if you can see your whole arm extended in front of you it's too low.

Is the follow-through the same for a cross-court and a down-the-line?

Yes, in the sense that the energy directing the racket head must be allowed to dissipate. But when you hit a ball cross-court you usually hit it a little earlier and the follow-through generally will extend across your body. When you hit down the line, you generally hit a little later and the follow-through will be more out in front of your body and, of course, in the direction the ball is traveling.

How firm should my wrist be when making contact with the ball?

As firm as possible without having it rigid. You should try to think of hitting from the shoulder, keeping your arm and wrist firm.

Should my wrist be traveling in front of or behind the racket face when I make contact?

When you make contact you want the face of the racket either even with the wrist or a little in front of it.

Should my feet be planted when I make contact with the ball?

Yes, whenever possible. A good way to check yourself is to hold out your racket at the end of a stroke. If you can keep your balance you know your feet were correctly set.

28

5.
GROUND
STROKES –
BACKHAND

Why do many pros say the backhand is easier than the forehand?

At the highest level of the game most players have better backhands than forehands because the backhand allows more power and accuracy with less effort. This is probably because the backhand is a more natural stroke—it calls for the arm to be flung out away from the body, which is a more natural movement than is required by the forehand, where the natural rhythm of the stroke carries the arm across and into the body.

What is the proper backhand grip?

I usually use an Eastern backhand grip with the handle of the racket held diagonally in my hand and my fingers comfortably spread.

What is the proper way to approach a backhand?

The four main components of your backhand and forehand are alike. They are:

1. Get into the ready position, keeping your eyes on the flight of the ball.
2. Turn or pivot, using the left hand to help take the racket back.
3. Step toward the net.
4. Follow through, from low to high.

Face the net in the ready position with the racket held directly in front of you, waist high and parallel to the ground. Your weight should be on the balls of your feet so that you feel tension in the calves of your legs. Be prepared to move either to the right or the left.

Concentrate. Don't watch your opponent or a spectator or the player in the next court. Watch the ball, especially from the time it leaves your opponent's racket and you then determine whether it is coming to your forehand or your backhand. As you move toward the ball, whether to your right or your left, remember to move sideways and into the ball, not sideways and backward.

Turn your entire body parallel to the flight of the ball. The turn will bring your racket to the center of your body or halfway back. During the remainder of the backswing your shoulders should be at right angles to the net.

After you have turned your body in the direction of the ball, your right arm is on the left side of your body, with the elbow tucked against your right hip, your shoulders and feet forming a plane perpendicular to the net.

From this position you should take the racket straight back without any loops or other frills, with the left hand lightly holding the throat of the racket to help guide or pull the racket into its proper position.

At the moment of maximum backswing your right arm is fully outstretched but the head of the racket does not reach back any farther than the imaginary extension of the plane. Actually, it is as though you were reaching with your right arm for something to the left and almost directly in back of you.

Use your knees as elevators, especially when you

have to get down for a low ball so that you can connect with the ball at waist level.

You should plan to hit the ball when it is 12 to 18 inches in front of your right leg. If you prepare properly and then move into the ball and hit it on the rise at waist level, you will make contact at the point of maximum power.

Keep your head down and your eyes on the ball right up to and beyond the moment of impact.

The wrist should be firm and the right arm nearly fully extended at the moment of impact. The farther away from your body you hit the ball, assuming you hit it in the pocket of your strings, the more power and accuracy you will gain.

You should feel a definite tension through your back as your body, in effect, coils when you bring back the racket and then uncoils as you swing forward and shift your weight from your rear foot to your front foot. The swing itself should be nearly level, with the racket head neither raised nor lowered during the forward part of the swing.

After making contact with the ball, hit out freely. The follow-through should be a long one with the racket head ending up pointed at right angles to the plane of your feet.

Where is the best place to make contact with the ball on a backhand?

Waist high and about a shoulder's width ahead of your front foot which, for most people, means early.

THE BACKHAND—Ready position, pivot, backswing, planting right foot and shifting weight forward, forward swing, and follow-through

How close to the body should the racket be on the backswing?

Imagine touching your thumb to a pocket on your left hip when you bring the racket back. You don't want to have too much space between the racket and the body because then you'll come around the ball instead of hitting through it.

What use is the left hand?

To help draw the racket back into position quickly, and for balance.

How can I hit different types of backhand shots?

To hit a top spin, keep your racket head level up until the moment of impact and then brush the racket over the top of the ball.

To hit a slice, also keep the racket head level until the moment of impact and then tilt the racket face backward a bit during the forward part of the swing.

In either case the most important element is a long, flowing follow-through. If you don't achieve this the top spin will degenerate into a looping fluff shot with no depth, and the slice will become a soft floater that hangs in the air.

How can I hit a flat backhand down the line?

The most important thing is to stay sideways when you make contact with the ball. The follow-through is like throwing the face of the racket toward the spot on the court where you want the ball to go.

Ground Strokes—Backhand

Why do I so often hit my backhands cross-court?

Chances are you are not preparing quickly enough. You then try to rush the stroke and end up hitting the ball too close to your body or you open your stance and turn too soon.

Why do I always seem to be late on my backhand?

You probably fall into the common error of trying to make contact with the ball just off your forward foot, as you do with a forehand.

Is it all right to run around my backhand?

If you want to improve your backhand you should not run around it. But if you want to win a point and your backhand is weak and there's enough time, then run around it. But be aware that you are covering for a weakness. Also, you have indicated to your opponent that your backhand is weak so you will probably end up having more shots hit there. The only time I might run around a backhand is when my opponent has hit a weak second serve and I see an opportunity to blast a forehand down the line.

How long should I keep my head down on the stroke?

You should keep your head down watching the ball until you have completed the full stroke.

Why do I so often tend to rise up on my toes after hitting a backhand?

Probably because you are too close to the ball or because you have lifted your head too soon in order to see the results of the shot. The momentum of the stroke, however, should bring you up on your toes after you have completed the shot.

What should I do after completing a backhand shot?

Return to the ready position and, if possible, to the center of the court.

Do you recommend that a beginner learn a two-handed stroke?

No. A two-handed stroke requires speedy footwork and it is difficult to hit a very low, wide ball with two hands. But two-handed strokes are somewhat in vogue today among younger players.

What are the steps in hitting a two-handed backhand?

Since I don't use one I can only report on what I have observed in watching Chris Evert.

When Chris approaches the ball she is usually well balanced with her eyes right on the ball. Her opening position is similar to that of most right-handed players who use single-handed strokes. She holds the racket lightly with her left hand to achieve a good backswing but instead of dropping her left hand when she makes contact, she hangs onto the racket with both hands on the forward swing and both hands play an equal part in the action. Her left arm and wrist come in strongly as hitting factors.

Unlike most players who have a solid stance with both feet planted firmly on the ground when they make contact, Chris's right foot leaves the ground at the moment of impact and the arc of her swing is far shorter than that of a player who uses a one-handed stroke. However, she does have a high follow-through with the racket pointing down the target line.

6.
GROUND
STROKES—
GENERAL

Why have I so often heard that a player is only as good as his ground strokes?

The ground strokes are the fundamental shots of tennis, and the most important. During a match you will hit more ground strokes, meaning balls which bounce on your side of the court, than all other shots combined. Return of service is your first shot on half the points you play, and unless you plan to spend all your time at net, which is unlikely, your ground strokes are going to determine whether you are a consistent tennis player or an erratic duffer.

With only an average service you can still survive with a good forehand and backhand. However, with a booming serve and only fair or weak ground strokes you will be defeated by any opponent with a well-rounded game.

What should be the ready position for playing from the baseline?

The head of the racket should be held about waist high and pointed directly in front of you, not to the right or the left. Your weight should be distributed equally on both legs and you should be on the balls of your feet.

Once you see to which side of you the ball is coming,

immediately start moving toward it, and by toward it I mean forward. A common fault of beginners is to run sideways and back when they move after a ball. At the very least run directly parallel to the net and preferably run parallel to and in toward the net. There may be times when a ball comes so deep you have to move back to avoid hitting it off your shoetops, but unless your opponent has hit a devastating shot you will usually have plenty of time to come in. It is easier for you to hit an attacking ground stroke. Learn this early. Bad habits are hard to break.

What is the best height at which to hit the ball?

Whether you move forward or back, hit the ball on the rise or at the peak of its bounce. Every ground stroke should be hit waist high, which is the level of maximum power and control. Moving quickly to where you can hit the ball on the rise almost guarantees that you will do this. Just thinking about it forces you to get into a position more rapidly, and that gives your opponent less time to prepare for the return.

If you have to bend, bend from the knees, not from the waist. For some reason most players, especially women, have difficulty doing this and bend mostly from the waist if they bend at all. They lose much of their power and balance by bending from the waist. Obviously you can't keep your back completely rigid, but your knees should be the primary elevators. If the ball bounces high, extend your legs and get up on the balls of your feet; if it bounces low, get down as low as necessary.

Should I attempt to aim each shot?

Yes. Once you reach the stage where you can hit your forehands and backhands with a degree of consistency, you should plan in advance where every one of your shots is going. I cannot emphasize this enough. Do it even in practice—if you spend all your practice time just hitting the ball down the middle and shallow, you may get temporary satisfaction but in a match you will find it difficult to aim for the corners with confidence, let alone hit them. Being able to place the ball with accuracy and speed is vital. Concentrate on direction and control right from the beginning.

Should I try for depth on every shot?

Ideally, every ground stroke should land approximately 3 feet from your opponent's baseline and 2 feet from his sideline. This of course is impossible, even for top players, but you should aim for the baseline with every shot. The baseline is a long way off and it's better to hit too long than too short.

Where is the best place to make contact with the ball?

When hitting a forehand you should make contact with the ball when it is just about even with your front foot.

On the backhand, however, you should make contact with the ball at about a *shoulder's width ahead of your front foot.* If you make contact with the ball just off the front foot, that's too late (although it's a common error).

Is it all right to choke up on the racket?

When you are first learning you may have better control if you occasionally choke up on the racket, but if you consider the shoulder as a fulcrum then every inch you can extend the racket will mean more power as well as more reach.

Under normal circumstances the racket should be grasped as close to the butt of the handle as possible.

How long should I keep my head down watching the ball after I have made a stroke?

For any ground stroke you should watch the ball until you actually see it leave the racket face.

Every time I hit a ball I can tell you exactly why I made the shot I intended or why I missed it and when I miss it it's generally because I didn't stay down on the ball long enough. I have a tendency to jump up as I hit the ball, but I know I must keep my head down, watching the ball until it has left the racket.

What is most important in ground strokes: pace or depth?

Depth is most important by all odds. If you can get pace and depth, right on. The only exception to this might be if you're playing against someone who doesn't like to run forward or bend down low, in which case you might hit a short ball to them.

Why is it that I so often seem to hit off balance?

That is usually from lack of preparation. Watch the pro players carefully and you will see that they have the racket back and are in position to hit the ball *before* it bounces; the inexperienced players tend to begin their preparation after the ball has bounced on their side.

How far behind the baseline should I normally stay?

That depends on the speed of the court. It's better to play farther back from the baseline so that you must go forward to hit the ball rather than backward.

What is meant by feel?

One day you will do everything almost perfectly: moving into the ball purposefully, with the racket face in the proper position, making contact smack in the pocket. There will be a solid thunk as the ball leaves your racket and you will be conscious of a tingling sensation all through your body. That's what's known as feel. Once you experience it you will have taken a big step toward becoming a good tennis player.

7.
THE SERVE

With my associates at Tennis America, I have spent much of the past two years examining traditional instruction techniques for the serve and experimenting with new concepts. We confirmed what we always knew to be true: the best serves have always been the simplest, with no jerks or gyrations to disrupt rhythm and destroy momentum. By eliminating or refining much of what has been accepted as instruction technique, we have evolved our own system that not only works for the beginner but has proved helpful to many advanced players.

Following are the steps for our Point-of-Contact (POC) method of serving:

1. Grasp the racket at the throat with your fingers spread along the bottom edge of the racket strings.

    Face forward with your weight on your back foot. Raise your elbow high and touch the middle part of your back with the racket head.

    Transfer your weight forward on your front foot, and at the same time fully extend your hand over your head to the right (if you are right-handed). Then stop, but keep your eyes on the racket head. When your body is extended fully, the point at which you have stopped is the point of contact, and you must think only about that POC.

    Rock back and forth, transferring your weight each time and stopping at the POC.

    After you have done this often enough so that you visualize where the POC is, gradually

THE POINT-OF-CONTACT
SERVE, Step 1 —
"Scratching your back"
with racket held at
throat, transferring
weight forward while
extending racket, full
extension at Point of
Contact

lengthen your grip on the racket handle until you are finally grasping the racket at the butt of the handle and scratching the small of your back with the racket head. You will automatically have assumed the correct grip.

2. Stand about 10 or 15 feet away from a fence.

   Grasp a ball lightly in the fingers of your left hand.

   Place the ball at the POC at the right height and the precise moment and hit the ball, keeping your eyes on the racket face and ball as they make contact.

   At this stage you are not concerned about hitting the ball with force because your swing should stop at the POC. You should be hitting up and out, without bending at the waist.

3. Repeat the exercise without the ball. But this time when you reach the POC start counting aloud slowly from one to six as you transfer your weight from the heel of your front foot, bringing the racket down and across your body so that the butt of the handle is facing your opponent.

   Start with the weight on the heel of your left foot and finish with the weight on the toe. Your right foot should not move and you should be in perfect balance.

   Now repeat the exercise with the ball, placing it to the right-hand side (if you are right-handed) and forward from the body at the POC. Again you should be hitting up and out, keeping your eyes constantly on the ball; if you don't see it you can't hit it.

4. When you start your serve, both hands should be at the same height or level. I recommend resting the throat of the racket on your left hand as you start the serve.

   Both hands should be at the same height or level as you go through the various stages of the serve to moment of impact.

THE POINT-OF-CONTACT
SERVE, Step 2—Back
and side views of
practicing serve with
ball against fence

The Point-of-Contact Serve, Step 3 — Front view of complete swing emphasizing follow-through and weight transfer

THE POINT-OF-CONTACT SERVE, Step 4 — Position of the hands before and during the toss

What are the various types of serve?

There are believed to be four popular serves: the American twist, the top spin, the slice, and the flat serve. I don't believe it's possible for anyone to hit a genuine flat serve because some slice or twist has to be imparted to the ball at the point of contact.

For an American twist, the point of contact is farther behind your head and farther to the right of your body than for the POC serve you have just learned. Actually, the American twist is like a sidearm pitch in baseball. You must hit up and out from the side of your body and finish on the same side (if you're right-handed, you finish on the right side). The American twist requires more energy than any other serve and it is often difficult to control, so I don't recommend it for beginners.

With a top-spin serve the POC is even higher than with the American twist. If you let the ball drop, it would hit you on the forehead. As the racket comes up from the scratching-your-back position to the POC, hit the ball on the side that's away from the net and, using your wrist, roll the face of the racket up and over the ball. This will provide the top spin that causes the ball to travel, in a high arc, deep into the service court, where it will bounce high.

To hit a slice serve, place the ball a little farther to the right, as with the top-spin serve, but during the forward part of your swing, just before the POC, turn your wrist slightly to the right and exaggerate the natural right-to-left motion of your normal swing.

The Serve

What is the difference between a first serve and a second serve?

Since you usually can afford to gamble with your first serve because you have one left, your second serve should be as near to infallible as you can make it, which is why I consider the second serve more important than the first. The object of the second serve is to reduce your margin of error and get the ball in play.

A second serve should have enough top spin so that it will clear the net by about 4 feet and land in the opposite service court with plenty of room to spare but with enough pace and depth so your opponent will have difficulty putting it away.

Which serve should I concentrate on as a beginner?

My feeling is that the beginner is better off not worrying about which serve to learn first. Learn the one that comes most naturally to you so you can count on it, and then go after the other serves.

What are the actual mechanics of serving?

One of the best ways to get an idea of the proper service motion is to take an old racket and actually hurl it into the opposite court. If you can do that you can learn to serve.

To put it another way, hitting a serve properly is like throwing a baseball or football. The only difference is you "throw" the tennis ball off the racket as an extension of your hand.

Once the racket is at the point of maximum backswing, you are fully wound up and coiled, ready to release all your strength and momentum.

You get to this position simply by taking the racket back and reaching over your right shoulder, scratching the small of your back with the racket head. If you do this properly, your elbow will be almost straight up in the air and you will feel a slight strain in your upper arm. Your back should be perfectly straight or arched slightly backward. Don't bend at the waist. When you start to come forward, everything should move at once. Now your natural momentum will carry you forward, so that at the moment of impact your right foot is on line with your left.

What is the proper follow-through for a serve?

Your body should be fully stretched out so that it presents nearly a straight line from the bottom of your feet to the top of your racket. The follow-through ends up on the left side of the body.

Some players have a tendency to finish their service on the right side, but if you wind up on that side it means you have not used your body to the fullest and whatever power you have generated has come almost totally from your arm.

Is there any shortcut to learning how to serve?

I don't think there are any shortcuts in life, let alone tennis. I strain my guts almost every time I go out on the court. It takes time and practice to be good at anything, and you always feel you can do better.

FOLLOW-THROUGH ON SERVE — Note straight line of body at moment of impact and final left position of racket head

What is the correct service grip?

It is the same as the grip for a Continental forehand, with the V formed by the thumb and forefinger pointed just a trifle to the left of where it was for the forehand. The fingers should be slightly spread apart.

Is the serving motion different for a short person?

No. Short as I am, by using my POC technique of serving and hitting up and out on the ball, I can serve effectively from my knees. The only alteration I make is in hitting up more on the ball and putting a little more top spin on it to bring it down into the court.

How should my weight be distributed for a serve?

The important thing is that you be comfortable and mobile with a solid base.

Should the point of contact be to the right, directly overhead, or to the left?

Slightly to the right. If you let the ball fall to the ground it should land about a foot to your right and about 2 feet in front of you. Practice the toss until you can place the ball in the air at the same spot every time.

PRACTICE TIP: Don't use a backswing. Place the racket in the scratching-your-back position, making certain your elbow is pointing high in the air, and proceed with the forward half of the swing. Hit the ball by using the full swing, keeping your feet planted firmly on the ground.

You may not generate much pace with this practice exercise but it's one of the best ways to establish what your racket will do during this part of the service, and it will help you become aware of balance.

Where is the proper place to stand for serving?

According to the rules, when you are serving into the deuce court you can stand behind the baseline anywhere from the center of the court to the right sideline. When serving into the ad court you can be anyplace from the center of the court to the left sideline. But by standing as near to the center of the court as possible, when serving into either court, you give yourself an advantage: you are in the center of the court and thereby able to cover both sidelines after your opponent makes his return. Also, you are in the best position to run forward to the net. Some players stand 6 to 8 feet away from the center line when they are serving. This gives them a better angle, but it also gives their opponent a better angle for the return and it leaves one sideline on the server's court totally unprotected.

How far behind the baseline should I stand?

Assuming you are right-handed, your left foot should be about 2 inches behind the baseline and your right foot should be about 12 inches behind it and about 4 inches to the right. A line connecting your feet would form a 60-degree angle to the baseline, placing you sideways to the net but facing it slightly.

Should I try for placement or an ace with my first serve?

Try for placement. You can expect a ball to come back but you can never anticipate an ace, so you must serve the ball where it will cause the most difficulty for your opponent.

Should I have a distinct first and second serve?

I suggest a happy medium; don't bomb the first serve and pitty-pat the second. Hit the first serve at three-quarter speed and take a little speed off the second, trying to give both serves reasonable depth and pace.

What is more important in a serve – depth or speed?

Depth! Most beginners, especially women, seem to have difficulty hitting a deep serve – that is, getting the serve to within 3 feet of the service line. If the ball lands shorter than that your opponent can take two leisurely steps forward and knock the ball past you for a winner.

This problem is caused by people being afraid to hit the ball too long, but a simple exercise will prove how difficult it is to do this. Sometime when you are practicing, try to hit the fence behind the opposite half of the court with a serve. You'll find it almost impossible.

When you are starting out don't be afraid to have your serves land a little behind the service line. That's better than having them hit the net. As with all other shots in tennis, once your serve is grooved it's much easier to shorten the length of it by 1 or 2 feet than it is to gain 1 or 2 feet of depth. The more depth you gain in your serve, the more time you have to follow it to the net and the less time your opponent has to get set for a return.

Where is the best place to aim a serve?

Most of the time you should serve to your opponent's weaknesses and avoid his strengths. This usually means serving to his backhand, but it is a good idea to surprise him occasionally with a serve to his strength.

The area you serve into is determined to a large extent by the angle available to you and the height of the net. At the center of the court the net is 3 feet high, but toward the sidelines it gradually increases until it reaches 3 feet, 6 inches. That extra 6-inch difference is something to keep in mind if you have a shaky serve. From the deuce court the majority of your first serves should be hit straight down the middle to your opponent's backhand, clearing the net at its lowest point.

Should I decide beforehand where I want to hit my serve?

Yes. This is true of every shot but particularly true of the serve because it's the only shot in which you are hitting the ball where you have placed it.

How can I get more power into my serve?

Power is built up from your first acceleration to the point of contact. It starts at the point of scratching your back as you hit up and out and it increases as you continue pushing through the ball after making contact.

Power is also obtained by anything else that gives you momentum through the point of contact, such as a snap of the wrist at the top of the serve.

How can I keep my opponent from anticipating the place I am going to serve to?

Start your swing the same way every time. Also, try not to look at the place you intend to serve to. You should train yourself to look at the same place each time before beginning a serve. I suggest looking directly at your opponent.

Should I start out serving hard?

By the time you actually start to play a game you should be completely warmed up and should have practiced your serve enough to be ready to go at full speed.

If there isn't time for you to warm up properly, however, you should run a little or do some exercises to get your muscles loose and your body moving.

The Serve

Should I follow a soft second serve to net?

That depends on the depth of the serve and the amount of spin you have imparted to it. If the serve is deep and has a lot of spin, it is probably safe to follow to net—unless you have served to your opponent's strength and you can see him about to tee off on it.

What can I do if I have to serve into the sun?

Vary the point of contact. Place the ball to the left or right so you can look up and around the edges of the sun.

Is it all right to serve underhand?

There's nothing in the rule book against it, and sometimes players do it for the purpose of surprise. If you have an injury that makes it impossible to raise your arms over your head then you must serve underhand.

What can I do if my first serve is consistently off?

Use your second serve and try for more spin, accuracy, and depth. When your second serve is going in with regularity you will have built up enough confidence to again try your first serve. But don't panic or despair when your first serve is off—and stays off. There are days like this in every pro player's life and that's why most of them have such reliable second serves.

When you go to your second serve, however, you must realize that you are in a more defensive situation, which means you must concentrate on getting your serve in deep, with accuracy, using spin to give you more margin for error.

How can I get my serve back on when it is off?

Generally there's a certain sameness to each player's problem when his serve is off. In my case, for example, my point of contact may be too low. On every serve I have to say to myself, "Get the ball up and out in front and stay on it."

What if I don't have any serve other than a pitty-pat?

Then try to pitty-pat your first one in a little harder, and if you can't hit it harder at least get it in deep.

Are there times when a soft serve is an advantage?

A soft serve can be an advantage against players who are accustomed to returning hard serves and who lose their rhythm when faced with a serve calling for them to generate their own power.

What should I do against an opponent who is constantly moving in on my second serve?

Try to get your first serve in more often, doing whatever is necessary to accomplish this.

8.
RETURN
OF SERVE

*Is it true that a good return of serve is one of the
most important strokes in tennis?*

Yes. A primary difference between a pro and a weekend player lies in the ability to return the serve accu-
rately. Return of serve is as important a part of the
game as serving. Much of the time a good return will
win you the point.

*What should I try to achieve with my service re-
turn?*

Primarily you want to get the ball in play. You should
move in before your opponent starts his service motion.
That way you put pressure on him before he starts the
point, and that little psychological edge is important.
   Keep in mind, however, that when you move in there
will be less distance between you and your opponent's
baseline, so you must adjust the depth of your return.

Does the server usually have the advantage?

Only if he has a good serve. In club or social play the
receiver often has the edge because he knows within
clearly defined limits where his opponent is going to hit
the ball and he can prepare himself mentally and
physically to make the most of that advantage. A prop-

erly executed return of serve is one of the most gratifying shots in tennis.

How should I prepare to return a serve?

Stand in the ready position with your weight on the balls of your feet and your racket held firmly in front of you at waist level and pointed straight out toward the net. A hard-hit ball generally comes low over the net, and there's no point in holding your racket high and then having to drop it as you start your swing. It's always easier to bring your racket up than to drop it.

When receiving service in the ad court many players like to cheat a little by setting their racket for a backhand return. If your opponent seldom hits to your backhand in the ad court it is better to take the normal ready position.

As soon as the ball leaves your opponent's racket and you know whether it is coming to your forehand or to your backhand you should turn from the waist and then take your racket back. If there's time you can then move your feet.

What grip should I use for return of serve?

Grip your racket for the shot you least like to hit. If your forehand is not as reliable as your backhand, wait for the service with a forehand grip. You want to do everything to make your weaker shot less difficult.

RETURN OF SERVE—Front view of forehand and
backhand from ready position to Point of
Contact; note racket head on backswing,
racket in relation to ground, grip in relation to
body, body in relation to net

What is the best way to return a hard serve?

It's essential to shorten your backswing as much as possible, but keep in mind that the follow-through is necessary if your return is to have pace and direction.

If you are playing on a fast court and the serve is hard, you can either slice your return or simply block it back: draw the racket back slightly and stick it out in front of the ball. If your wrist is firm and the contact is solid you should make a good shot. Most important of all, try to keep the ball in play.

Where is the best place to stand for returning the serve of a right-hander?

When a right-hander serves to you, he carries the racket across his body from right to left, causing the ball to drift to your right. If he serves you an extreme slice, the ball may carry as much as 8 or 10 feet to your right.

So when a right-hander serves to you in the deuce or right-hand court you know the ball will tend to drift to the right. Since you want to be equidistant from the two extremes of the ball's flight, I suggest you stand on the baseline, bisecting the angle. In effect, the nearer the server stands toward the center, the nearer you move toward the center. The wider he stands, the wider you stand.

At first it may seem that you are giving away some ground but in fact by bisecting the angle you have equal distance to cover on both sides.

In this way you also tempt your opponent to go for the perfect serve down the middle, putting increased pressure on him.

A right-hander's serve to the left-hand court, or ad court, usually will drift to the right. This lessens the likelihood of a ball coming in wide to the left, so you should position yourself about 3 feet from the left sideline. You will again by equidistant from the ball's two extreme lines of flight.

Where is the best place to stand to return the serve of a left-hander?

A left-hander's service motion will cause the ball to drift in the opposite direction from a right-hander's serve. In the deuce court you should stand about 1 foot closer to the center than you would in receiving a right-hand service; your left foot should be on the left-hand service line.

A left-hander's serve to your right generally goes to your forehand. So if the ball is going into your body, it's usually easier to try to take the shot on your backhand.

What is the best way to handle a top-spin serve?

Either take it very early, before the spin has a chance to develop, or take it very late when the spin has had time to wear out. It's best to take it early if you can.

Where is the best place to return a serve in singles?

That depends on whether the person is coming in or staying back. If the server is a net rusher the most difficult shot for him to handle, particularly if he's tall, is a shot that bounces off his shoe tops.

If the server is staying back you generally want to hit the return cross-court and deep.

Should I move in on a second serve?

That depends, of course, on how hard and deep your opponent hits his second serve. If you know that the serve is going to be soft it is wise to move in 2 or 3 feet, thereby throwing the server a bit off balance and putting yourself in a more offensive position.

Is there any way to psych out a server?

Yes. If the server is hitting consistently to your backhand you can wait until he throws up the ball for the serve; then, at the last moment, run around your backhand. Or you can stand very wide, making it apparent that you are ready for a backhand serve. Both these devices put pressure on the server to attempt to hit the ball to your forehand.

You can also move in a couple of steps, making certain the server sees that you are standing close and thus forcing him to make a mental and a physical adjustment. By forcing him to think about where he is going to hit the ball you have put pressure on him and interrupted his rhythm and, possibly, his concentration.

Do you have a strategy in mind before returning service?

Yes. I usually decide in advance what I am going to do with the ball before it reaches me.

Is power or control more important in returning service?

Control. When you learn how to hit through the ball properly you can add power. Most people will find it easier to add power to control than to add control to power.

Should I hit a service return as I would hit a ground stroke?

Yes, but with a shorter backswing.

Is it all right to run around my backhand on the second serve and take it on my forehand?

There usually isn't time. In any event I don't advise it — you might as well take the serve on your backhand because your backhand will have to improve eventually.

Should I return a second serve with as much pace as I do a first serve if the server is coming to net?

On a second serve the ball is coming to you slower, so you have more time to get into position and prepare yourself for a good return, as you would for a normal ground shot. Since you have the advantage you should try to attack a second serve whenever possible. If you can't go for a winner then hit the return slow and straight at your opponent's feet, forcing him to bend over and put his own pace on the ball. By hitting the return softly you have time to get into good position for his return.

Should I mix up my returns?

Yes. You want to keep your opponent from anticipating where you are going to hit the ball. But above all you must get the ball back over the net and in play.

9.
NET PLAY –
VOLLEYS

Do you consider a good volley necessary?

Indeed I do. The volley is the most efficient shot in tennis and should be considered a prime offensive weapon for furthering your attack.

What is the proper grip for the volley?

Most pros use a slightly different grip for almost every shot. I suggest that even beginning players change grips, too, if there's time. If there isn't enough time you may want to use just one grip for the volley, in which case I suggest the Continental forehand grip, same as for the serve.

How much of a backswing is needed for a volley?

Hardly any. You don't really swing for a volley. Beginners have a tendency to take a full backswing for a volley, as they would for a ground stroke, but if you learn from the beginning to punch your volleys you will never have to worry about breaking a bad habit. The racket moves no more than 2 feet before it makes contact with the ball.

The shorter the swing, the more control you have of the racket head. Most of the power you need for an effective volley comes from your opponent's shot; you can easily supply the rest with your 2-foot swing, and much of the time you won't have the opportunity to take that.

How much follow-through should a volley have?

The ball should stay on the racket strings for at least 6 inches, which is time enough to give it direction and control. You don't slap at a volley any more than you do at a ground stroke.

What is the most important thing to remember about a volley?

Always try to get distance and power and, if possible, hit the ball where your opponent isn't or, as the late Vince Lombardi would say, hit to daylight. People used to ask me why I volleyed so well. It's something I never thought much about but just did. I finally realized that my conception of the volley is to hit up and out, which is why it's so good.

What is the ready position for volleying?

Basically it's the same ready position as for return of service, with the racket pointed directly in front of you about waist high and level with the ground. You want to remember that when a ball is fast it's generally low. This gives you less time to prepare for it, so it's wiser to keep the face of the racket a little lower. For example, I hold the racket a little below waist level so I can be ready for a fast ball. When the ball is higher it's generally slower, so I have time to bring the face of the racket up to hit the ball.

You should stand on the balls of your feet with your weight equally distributed on both legs and slightly forward. From this position you are prepared to move in any direction.

What is the problem most people have with volleying?

Most people swing too much or try to do too much with their volleys. At our tennis camps we instruct beginners to use just their hands, teaching them to try to catch the ball in front of them, that way they develop their hand and eye coordination. The trick is to try to catch the ball with your racket but with a firm wrist.

How far toward the net should I run before stopping and preparing for a volley?

Run forward as far as you can until you see that your opponent is about to hit the ball, then make one little jump forward so you end up in the ready position with your weight equally distributed on both feet. You can now move either to the right or to the left.

The cardinal rule of a good volley is to get as close to the net as possible, thus opening up more potential angles for your return and cutting down on the possibilities of hitting your volleys into the net.

After making a first volley, when should I retreat from the net?

After the first volley, wherever it may be, you should always move forward. Never stand still or retreat. Every foot you move forward from inside the service line increases tremendously the angles available to you, and the sharper the angle, the greater your chances of hitting a put-away.

As you advance, however, remember to stop your forward movement completely at the moment when your opponent hits his return shot. You don't want to be caught moving in a particular direction, committing yourself, until you know where your opponent is going to hit the ball.

Should I rush the net even if I have a weak volley?

If you have a weak volley it's silly to rush the net, just as it's foolish to stay on the baseline when you have a slashing volley. You have to know what kind of game you want to play, or simply play your best and capitalize on your strength and protect your weakness. But without a good volley it will be difficult for you to play first-class tennis.

Should I swing level or hit down on the volley?

Hit up and out.

At what height should I hit a volley?

If possible, volleys should not be hit lower than at waist level.

What should I do on a low volley?

Bend from the knees, not from the waist, and keep your wrist firm. The face of your racket should automatically open a little and you must remember to hit up and out.

What is the best way to handle a shoulder-high volley?

This presents the same problems as a low volley, only in reverse. A volley hit above the height of the shoulders, especially on the forehand side, is difficult because you have too much time to hit the ball and you tend to lose your rhythm; instead of swinging by instinct and reflex you must stand and wait for the ball. Also, a high volley is difficult because a ball hit at about shoulder height can't be hit with much power in either the horizontal or vertical plane.

So the first thing you should do is try to get under the ball and take it as an overhead. But whatever you do, don't hit down on the ball. Hit straight through it and unless you are Hercules or an amazon your ball will land in your opponent's court with plenty of room to spare. Take a little more backswing, keeping your wrist extremely firm and hitting the ball flat.

When you get such a volley it's a good chance to move in as quickly as possible, even if you end up on top of the net before you start your swing. If you get in that close, even the most awkward shot can be turned into a winner.

HITTING A LOW VOLLEY—
Note bending of knees,
open face of racket
throughout, and short
swing

How should I handle a wide volley?

The problem with a wide volley is that you have to stretch out to meet the ball, which reduces the power of your return. You must hit up and out on the ball even if you have to take a slightly longer backswing. Keep your wrist firm no matter how far you have to reach, and hit the ball as far in front of you as possible.

When should I try to hit a volley down the line?

That depends on the height of the ball. If it is at waist height or lower you should try to hit down the line because then you are in a better position for the next volley.

What are the differences in handling a volley to the backhand and a volley to the forehand?

When your opponent has hit the ball and you have determined where it is going, don't wait for the ball to come to you. Turn your body in the direction of the ball.

If the ball is coming to your right, turn and step forward and across your body with your left foot. Don't step backward with your right.

If the ball is coming to your backhand, turn and step forward and across with your right foot.

You want to hit the ball as far in front of you as possible because you have a better chance of seeing it. Ideally, you should hit a forehand volley about a foot ahead of your left leg, and a backhand volley about a shoulder's width ahead of your right leg.

HITTING A WIDE VOLLEY —
Note stretch and hitting
up off back foot

How can I handle a volley hit directly at me?

The instinct of self-defense will help you a lot more than you think. When a ball is hit directly at you the natural instinct is to get out of the way or get your racket in front of you. If the ball is hit so hard you can't get out of the way, you should bring your racket in front of you in the backhand position. Since you can't take a backswing, you should concentrate on meeting the ball solidly and angling your return sharply.

When volleying against an opponent at net, what should I watch for?

You should try to anticipate where he is going to hit because when both of you are at the net the distance between you is very short and you will have very little time to read the ball or cover it. You should try to come back to the ready position each time you make a shot so that you are prepared to go in any direction.

What is the most difficult volley for an opponent to handle?

A shot hit directly at his right hip or directly at his feet.

10.
NET PLAY—
LOBS

Do you consider it important for a beginner to learn how to lob?

Indeed I do. Most people don't realize that a lob is one of the most valuable and frequently used shots in tennis and even pro players must have it in their repertoire. I practice my lobs every day.

What kind of stroke should I use for a lob?

Use a full stroke without quite as much backswing but a long follow-through. Try to step into the shot as though you were hitting a ground stroke.

What is the difference between an offensive lob and a defensive lob?

An offensive lob is used to push your opponent away from the net and a defensive lob is used when you are in trouble and have been taken wide off the court by your opponent's shot and want to get back into position.

THE LOB – Note long
follow-through

Where is the best place to aim an offensive lob?

Over your opponent's backhand side. You should hit an offensive lob from inside the baseline on a low trajectory but a little higher than your opponent can reach with a slight jump.

Where is the best place to aim a defensive lob?

As near to your opponent's baseline as possible. Most people should try to lob diagonally across the court because they will then be hitting into the longest part of the playing area, giving themselves a better chance to keep the ball in bounds.

Should I rush to the net after making an offensive lob?

No, because your lob will probably be returned as an overhead smash. The best position for you to take after making a defensive lob is about 3 feet behind the baseline.

How should I handle a defensive lob?

Most pros try to take them in the air, but I recommend that as a beginning player you let the ball bounce first. There is less likelihood that you will mistime and mishit the ball as it is coming down.

If you do try to take a lob in the air remember to hit up and out, not down.

When should I not lob?

When you have a chance of making an easy passing shot or put-away.

Should I return a lob with a lob?

It's better to hit a lob with an overhead whenever possible because that gives you a chance for a put-away shot, and even if you don't put the ball away you have at least put your opponent on the defensive.

If you have to run back to get the ball you are wiser lobbing it back to get your opponent away from the net. Try to hit the ball as deep in his court as possible.

What is the best offense against a persistent lobber?

A good overhead.

What can I do with a lob that is going to land some distance behind me?

Try to run far enough ahead of the ball so that you can pivot and take it on your forehand. If your opponent hasn't come to the net you should try to return the lob as a regular ground stroke.

How can I handle high top-spin lobs?

Try and catch a top-spin lob before it bounces, remembering to hit up and through the ball. If that's not possible, you should get back farther than usual because the rotation of the ball will cause it to bounce deeper into the court.

If you can take a top-spin lob as an overhead, great, but most inexperienced players are probably wiser taking it on the forehand. The trick here is to try and judge the way the ball will bounce, so you are waiting for it. Keep your stroke short and simple and hit flat through the ball.

11.
NET PLAY—
OVERHEADS

What are the steps in hitting an overhead?

The first thing to do is turn sideways to the flight of the ball and get your racket in back of you as in the scratching-your-back position. Then hit the ball as you would a serve: up and out, not down. Never think down.

Should I take an overhead in the air or let it bounce when possible?

If you think the ball is going to bounce on the service line or in front of it, take it in the air. If you think it's going to land behind the service line or there is sun or wind, let it bounce.

Where is the best place to aim an overhead?

Aim an overhead smash down the center of the court. A smash is difficult enough to control without trying for angles.

Where is the most likely place an overhead will be returned?

In Australia I was taught that nine times out of ten most right-handed players hit to the right side of their

THE OVERHEAD — Note position of anticipation sideways to flight of ball, full extension of body, and hitting "up and out"

body and left-handers hit to the left because it's physically easier to hit to your natural side than to come across your body with the racket.

PRACTICE TIP: A good way to learn how to hit overheads is to have one hit to you and then run back without a racket and try to catch the ball in your right hand, keeping your arm in front of you. Then switch to the racket and hit the ball out in front of you.

12.
GENERAL
QUESTIONS
ON SINGLES

What is the most important element in strategy?

To understand your game. Most people try to understand their opponent's game and not their own.

In order to play tennis to the maximum of your ability, you have to know your own strengths and weaknesses. Then in a game situation you must constantly try to capitalize on your strengths and protect against your weaknesses.

And you must know your emotions. How do you hold up under pressure? How do you react when you're ahead? Can you make a kill when you have a chance? Do you think of yourself as a winner or a loser?

Do you always play to win?

Always. In my view, the key to tennis is competing. In competition someone has to win and I want it to be me or my side. I will beat an opponent 6-love if I can and even if I outclass my opponent I'll play every point as though it is match point without letting up.

I believe it does a player harm to clown around on the court, so I make every shot count. I want every shot to be a winner or else my rhythm is thrown off. I always keep working toward the ultimate: the perfect shot.

Is there any truth to the saying that whoever wins the most first points of a match usually wins the match?

Some recent surveys indicate that this is so. When I am serving, I know it's particularly important to me to win the first serve.

Are you upset when you lose your first service in a set?

No, but it doesn't help to know that I must take my opponent's serve in order to remain in the match.

How do you feel about losing?

I'm a terrible loser. I know I can lose but I don't like to accept it, and why should I? Some people get discouraged by losing but it fires me up, and if I lose a game I replay it over and over in my head, feeling mad and miserable but determined that the next time I play that person I'm not going to make the same mistakes.

Are you nervous before a big match?

I'm always nervous or psyched up before any match.

How can I psych myself up when I'm tired or tense?

Every player has his own system. I get angry with myself, call myself names, and goad myself into playing better. I like tension. It makes me perform better.

Most of us get tentative with our strokes when we are tense, and we don't follow through as much. To get out of a bad run, I hit through the ball, lay into it hard a few times and hit out.

Often, when you double fault or get uptight, your mind starts to wander and you lose your concentration; you think ahead to the future and fear double faulting, so you live up to your anticipation. The best thing to do is take a positive approach and think of yourself hitting a serve or stroke successfully.

Do you have any suggestions to help me improve my concentration on the court?

Practice yoga or meditate quietly before a game if that helps you.

On a crucial point I concentrate even harder by pretending that I am down. If I'm ahead 5-3, I switch it around in my head so I'm behind and say to myself I have to win the next game to stay in the match. I concentrate like fury on each point, telling myself it's match point.

One thing I can tell you with certainty is that you should not concentrate on your opponent. Concentrate on the ball!

Must I disguise my shots?

You should try to disguise your shots as much as possible by preparing for each shot in the same way and by hitting the ball at the last moment. Normally, however, only a pro can disguise his shots effectively.

Disguise should be attempted only after you have reached an advanced level of play.

Is it important to develop a bread-and-butter shot?

Everyone has one shot that is his best, a shot that he can count on most of the time. Champions try to make their weak strokes at least adequate, but they all have one great shot which is what helped make them champions.

Most people think my bread-and-butter shot is my volley, but I think it is any stroke on my backhand side. If my backhand is off I'm in trouble.

Is it better to simply keep the ball in play or to occasionally try for a winner?

That depends on you as a person. If you feel tentative on the court then you should try to be bolder, but if you are the aggressive type who constantly bombs the ball you should try to be more accurate.

Do you pace yourself when playing?

If I ever had to pace myself I'd have to quit, because that is not my style. The only way I can play is to go all out on every point, which is why I've always had to be in good shape. I've had two knee operations and I've gone through a lot of matches when I haven't been physically up to par. And generally those are the times I have lost.

What is the key to percentage play?

Don't take unnecessary risks. And go for a winner only when you feel you can make it.

What usually determines where you will hit the ball?

Whenever possible, I try to hit to daylight.
The average club player, however, usually makes certain shots at certain times because it's physically easier to hit the ball to a particular location on the court. It's unimportant that your opponent may know where the ball is going. If it's hit properly, the chance of winning the point is that much greater.

Do you watch your opponent when you are playing?

To a certain extent, but I try to play the ball, not my opponent.

What is the most common mistake you make when playing?

When I miss a shot it's generally because I don't stay down on the ball long enough. I tend to let the ball get too close on my forehand side and, to compensate, I have a tendency to jump up as I make contact. This is a bad habit I share with some other top players, like Rod Laver.

What are the most important points in a game?

All points are important, but the so-called break points are in ad games when the score is 40-30 or 30-40. When the ad is in your favor, you only need one point, but when you're down an ad it takes three points to win the game.

Should women play a different kind of game than men?

No, good tennis is good tennis regardless of sex. Sometimes women have to work more on technique and timing because they aren't able to muscle the ball over as readily as men do.

How do you handle bad calls?

I always try to ignore them so it doesn't affect my concentration.

What do you do when you feel you're losing your temper?

I know that I am quick-tempered. I have had to learn to control my temper and direct it properly. When I do that I'm right on.

Billie Jean King's Secrets of Winning Tennis

Is there more tension in a sudden-death play-off than in a game?

Yes. It's great, though, and I love it. It's the pressure, man, and that's where it's at for me.

What do you do when you change sides?

That's a very important sixty seconds in my life and I use that time to get myself together.

13.
DOUBLES—
SERVING | *Your First Serve*

Where is the best position for me to stand when serving in doubles?

About halfway between the center of the court and the singles sideline. That way you are dividing responsibility for coverage of the court between you and your partner and, at the same time, you are dividing your opponents' possibilities in half. From that midway position you can reach just about any ball hit crosscourt, including an extreme angle shot.

Is it all right for me to go wide and stand nearer to the sideline?

No, because it is almost impossible for you to serve the ball down the center from that position. Also, by standing wide you signal to the receiver that your serve will probably be wide and he will be prepared for it.

What should be my primary thought when serving in doubles?

Get the first serve in deep.

Where is the best place for me to aim my first serve?

Straight at your opponent because he has to get his body out of the way to make the return and you cut down his possibilities for making an angled return.

Should I try for an ace with my first serve?

Not unless you are in a position where you can afford the gamble. It's far wiser to use a medium-paced, deep serve and move it around as much as possible so your opponent cannot get set for his return.

When I serve in doubles I usually hit my first serve with a lot of spin, giving me assurance that it will get in deep.

Should I rush to the net after my first serve?

That depends on the serve and how much trouble it is causing the receiver. If it's deep and well placed you should try to get to the net to put pressure on the receiver because when you are at the net or going to it you are in an offensive position.

Should I wait to see if the serve is in before going to the net?

If you are serving properly and making contact with the ball when it is in front of you, you will automatically be hitting and falling forward after making contact. That momentum is what helps you start toward the net for your first volley.

What can I do if I am unable to get to the net after serving?

Retreat a step or two behind the baseline to the position you normally take when rallying.

If I haven't started toward the net after serving when should I start?

At the first opportunity, which will generally come when one of your opponents hits a short return.

Your Second Serve

Do I serve from the same position?

Yes.

Is there anything I can do about getting choked up?

What usually makes people choke on any stroke is thinking about the past instead of the future. If you've missed with your first serve that's no reason for you not to get your second serve into the court. You must have a positive approach to your second serve because the moment you approach it negatively, you're lost.

Why is it considered such a cardinal sin to double fault?

Because you give your opponent the point. More than 80 percent of the points in tennis are lost through errors, rather than won by placements. Every time you force your opponent to hit the ball, the odds increase in your favor.

What should I try to achieve with my second serve?

To get the ball over the net deep and in the service court, even if you have to pitty-pat it.

Is there any place I should aim a weak second serve?

The best percentage shot when you are serving into the deuce court is down the middle to the receiver's backhand, if your opponent is right-handed, because you give him less angle on the return and have a better chance to make a play.

When serving to the ad court a soft serve hit deep to his backhand may prove troublesome for your opponent.

Should I always try to hit my second serve to my opponent's backhand?

Not always. The reason most people hit a second (or first) serve to their opponent's backhand is because that usually elicits a weaker response. It's a good idea to hit to your opponent's weaknesses but you should not forget to occasionally hit to his strength, if for no other reason than to keep him from getting set.

Should I follow a soft second serve to the net?

That depends on how good the receiver is. If he blasts your second serves there's no point in following them to the net.

What if I am unable to place my second serve?

Get it in as deep as possible and work on your first serve. Even if your first serve isn't deep, it is likely to be more effective than a weak and haphazard second serve.

What can I do if my opponent constantly moves in on my second serve?

Try to get your first serve in more often.

Does a left-handed server have an advantage over a right-handed receiver?

Yes, because there are fewer left-handers playing the game, so right-handers are not as accustomed to the curve coming in the opposite way.

Your Partner Serves

Where should I stand?

Most social players stand too far in the alley and too close to the net, thus giving the opposing receiver too much open space on the server's side of the court. Whenever possible, when your partner is serving, you should stand almost in the middle of the box, thus dividing your obligation for court coverage into equal parts.

You can, of course, vary this position from time to time. You can act as though you are going to stand in the middle and then feint to one side or the other, trying to get the receiver to hit to a position he thinks you have vacated.

Should I keep the same position for both serves?

Yes.

Where is the best place for me to return the first volley?

If the ball comes to you at shoulder height, hit it to the feet of the man who is nearest to you. If the ball comes to you low, volley it to the man farthest from you or volley it down the center. If both of your opponents are in the backcourt, volley as deep as possible.

When should I poach?

Only when you think you can put the ball away.

Is it all right to poach on my backhand side?

That depends on the effectiveness of your backhand volley. Much of the time a return that you poach on the backhand can be handled more effectively by your partner because the ball is probably going to his forehand as he is coming into position after serving.

Should I poach on my forehand when my partner is serving to the deuce court?

The same rule of thumb applies: only poach if you are reasonably certain you can put the ball away. Whenever you poach, you leave your side of the court unprotected.

Is it better to poach off the first serve or the second?

If you are going to poach it's usually wiser off the first serve because your opponent is probably not as well prepared for his return and your answer. A second serve is generally hit slower and the receiver is in closer, which means he may be able to run around a serve to his backhand and take it on his forehand. If he sees you start to move he will probably hit down your alley.

What if my partner has a weak serve and I am getting bombed at the net?

Go back to the baseline halfway between the sideline and the center of the court. As soon as your opponents hit a weak shot you should move up. In any event, when you are playing back you should move up and back with your partner.

What should I do when my partner serves wide?

Hit wide to the receiver covering your alley.

What can I do to assist a partner who does not come to the net after serving and continually flubs all returns to his backhand?

Try to poach a few times to make your opponents aware that you are a force to contend with. Even if you miss the poach your opponents will still be wary because they know you may try it.

When your partner is serving to the deuce court, you might move closer to the center line, trying to force the receiver to hit cross-court to your partner's forehand.

When he is serving to the ad court, you might try playing Australian style. You stand just to the left of the center service line and your partner serves from the center of the baseline trying to hit to the backhand of the receiver. This technique forces your opponents to hit directly at you at the net or down the line to your partner's forehand or to try a lob over your head.

If you try the Australian technique, your partner must move immediately to his right after he serves in anticipation of a return to his forehand.

When my partner serves, whom should I be watching?

You should watch the receiver, and when the ball is in play you should keep your eyes on the person who is nearest to the net. When he starts to move, you will have advance warning to prepare for a shot that may come in your direction.

Return of Serve

Where is the best place to stand for return of service?

That depends on where the server is standing. You want to bisect the angle of the two extreme limits for the ball to come into the service court.

How should my partner and I determine who is to take which side?

That should depend on the relative strengths and weaknesses of each partner.

The accepted rule is for the weaker player to be in the deuce court with the stronger player in the backhand court because most players have better forehands than backhands and most serves into the deuce court are to the forehand. Also, there's a theory that if the weaker player keeps losing his deuce point, the stronger partner is still more likely to save the game. Personally, I prefer to play in the ad court because I am stronger on the backhand side, but if my partner has the weaker backhand I play the deuce court.

Is it better for the lefty to play in the ad or deuce court?

Again, that depends solely on ability. When a right-hander is teamed with a left-hander they normally start with the forehands down the middle because so many shots in doubles come down the middle.

Where should I attempt to return the serve?

The simplest return is one that is hit cross-court a shade to the left or right of the net's midpoint.

Another effective return is a ball hit slow and low at the server's feet. This is one of the most difficult shots for the onrushing server to handle and the op-posing netman probably won't be able to do much with it.

A third possibility is to return the ball as a lob over the netman's head. If it's hit high and deep enough it will force the server to cross over and answer with a backhand which usually results in an exceedingly weak shot.

You can also try to hit down the line hoping to catch the netman moving in the wrong direction or on the way to intercept what he thought was going to be a cross-court shot. You must remember, however, that the net is a full 6 inches higher at the sidelines than it is in the middle of the court and unless you can handle the serve easily, the odds are against your making a successful down-the-line shot. The margin for error is considerable.

102

Should I return a serve the same way in doubles as in singles?

No. In doubles the best return is usually a low, shallow cross-court. To make such a return you don't need as much backswing, which means you can stand closer in than you would in singles. This will also enable you to follow your return to the net, which is where you want to be as much as possible in doubles.

What can I do if the opposing net man is an effective poacher?

Lob a few returns well over his head at the very beginning of the set. If that doesn't work, hit down the line a few times forcing him to be a little more cautious about leaving his position. He may pick off your liners but you'll have given him something to worry about.

What should I do if the net man is effective and the server stays back rather than goes to the net?

Hit your return deep to the server and get to the net, or lob over the net man and go to the net.

Where is the best place to return a serve if I am unable to do much with it?

The best place is right at the feet of the server as he comes in.

What is the most important point in doubles?

Nobody can win a match without breaking service. Successful return of a serve rates as a key factor in winning matches. By getting the ball in play, you advance your chances of breaking service by 50 percent.

14.
DOUBLES—
NET PLAY

How close should I get to the net?

The closer you are to the net, the less territory you can cover. Most social players, especially women, tend to play too close to the net. I think there are two reasons for this: they may get a feeling of security from having the net so near at hand but, more important, it demands less skill at volleying. It's more than likely that a play close to the net will mean an opportunity to hit down on the ball, which is an easy thing to do because even a blocking stroke or tentative hit will usually keep the ball in play.

The shorter you are, the closer you must get to the net because you have less time to cover the ball. That's why a short person has to be in better shape than a tall person. I can move faster off the dime than Margaret Court, and I have quicker hands and reflexes, but she can cover a lot of court area with just a few steps. So I have to make up for my lack of size with my lateral movement and shot production.

The problem is that if you're too close to the net, a hard drive will flash by before you can react and you will also find it difficult to retreat, even for a short lob that could be converted into an overhead.

Where is the best place to stand at net?

The best place is about the middle of the service box where you can move forward or back easily and quickly. If you poach and cross the center service line, keep on going.

Where should the net man be looking?

He should watch the ball except when his partner is serving. When I am at net I always try to glimpse what my partner is doing and then I watch the ball while it is in play, keeping a close eye on the opponent nearest to me. If he doesn't react when my partner has hit a shot, I shift my attention to the other opponent. But I always watch the ball.

Which opponent should I concentrate on when I am at the net?

You should have the feeling of seeing both opponents, but generally you want to watch the person who is receiving.

When all four people are at the net what is the best shot to try?

Usually a slow shot is better than trying to power past your opponents. Hit the ball slow and low, forcing them to hit their return up so that you can then hit your return down and hard.

When my partner dinks a return and the net man is going to drive it down my throat, what can I do?

Duck.

Where is the best place to hit a volley?

It's usually safer to hit to the player who is farthest from you because you have more time to recover and get back in position for the next shot.

What can I do at the net to help out if my partner and one of the opposition are hitting deep drives to each other?

You should try to move in on a ball that has been returned somewhere within your range. The fact that you are at the net, alert and waiting to pounce, puts the opposing player under some pressure, but you must be careful to wait until your opponent has committed his shot so he does not detect your plan in advance and hit to the place you have just left.

What should I do when my partner hits a high lob?

Retreat behind the baseline as quickly as possible, anticipating an overhead smash from your opponents. Actually it would be a good idea if your partner told you in advance that he was going to hit a lob by shouting the word "back" so you can get moving. If the lob is deep and your opponents must run back to get it, then you and your partner should move in to the net.

Should I always try to smash a lob?

Yes.

15.
MIXED
DOUBLES

What do you think of mixed doubles?

It's like sex—it can be great if you have the right partner.

Is there any difference between social mixed doubles and competitive mixed doubles?

Anytime four people are on the court it's competitive. In social mixed doubles, however, the woman is frequently the weaker player and the man tends either to patronize her or try to blast her off the court. In professional doubles the men don't allow their women opponents any quarter. They play all out, which is the way pro tennis should be played.

Assuming that the woman is the weaker partner, what should she do?

She should make the same concessions that the weaker player usually makes in a doubles game. She should let her partner run back for the overhead smashes; she should not poach unless she is certain of putting the ball away; she should do everything possible to get her first serve in deep without too much angle, which opens up her side of the court; she should not double fault; and she should let her partner take almost every volley within his reach. She should also expect to be the target for most of the opponents' shots if they are determined to win.

How can a woman who is a weak player enjoy mixed doubles?

By playing her best game with emphasis on keeping the ball in play.

Have you any suggestions for a husband and wife team?

This is not a good idea because one of the pair is usually a better player and will start to offer criticism, especially if the team is losing. When that happens the couple ends up by fighting each other instead of their opponents.

What if the woman is the stronger player and plays opposite her husband?

That depends on how much she wants to win. If it's a serious match the woman has to think of her husband as an opposing player but not as an enemy. In any event, it's not a good idea for one spouse to embarrass the other on the court.

In his book *Winning Tactics for Weekend Tennis*, Tony Trabert offers some advice for couples which bears repeating. Tony suggests that before the match a husband and wife agree, "We're on opposite sides of the net and this is a competitive match. You really can't ask for any quarter on the tennis court but remember no matter who wins I love you and we're going home together."

In mixed doubles should the man or the woman take the overheads?

The person to take the overheads is the person who is standing nearest to the ball as it comes down, unless, of course, that person has no ability with an overhead. But the determining of who takes it should have nothing to do with the player's sex, especially if the woman is the stronger player.

16.
GENERAL
QUESTIONS
ON DOUBLES

What is the basic strategy in doubles?

The idea is to move to the net where you can volley with extreme angles on your side, or you can keep the ball deep. You and your partner should always move parallel to one another, never allowing the space between you to open up for a drive down the middle.

Should my partner and I make an agreement in advance about strategy?

This is difficult to do consistently, but it's always a good idea to have a battle plan.

It surprises me how often players, when they have a set weekly game in which they are partners, neglect to talk over the games beforehand or hold a critique afterward. Housewives swap recipes or gossip; businessmen talk about their work or gossip. Why not talk about the weaknesses and strengths of your tennis opponents and how you can capitalize on them?

Is it a good idea to hit down the middle to your opponents?

Yes, because most social players neglect to agree in advance on who will take balls that come down the middle and by the time they have turned and looked at each other, they have lost the point.

I keep hearing that doubles partners should move in tandem. What is meant by that?

It's important that partners move up and back together and sideways together so each one covers an equal area of the court.

How do we determine which area to cover?

You must always cover for the shortest distance between the opponent who is hitting the ball and yourself.

Is it all right to talk to my partner during a game?

Know your partner. Some people get uptight if you talk to them during a game and other people keep up a running conversation. But you should always be prepared to say "mine" or "yours" and warn him to fall back if you are going to hit a lob. If you do talk to your partner you should offer him encouragement and not criticism. No one fluffs or misses a shot deliberately and criticism will generally make them more insecure.

Who should take a ball down the middle in doubles?

That sort of agreement should be reached before starting the game. Normally, the person on the forehand takes it. On the other hand, when Karen Susman and I played together our backhands were so much stronger than our forehands that we agreed that the person in the forehand court should play the shot down the middle. And, since I played the forehand court when I was teamed with her, I took almost every volley down the middle.

What is the most important area of the court to cover in doubles?

The obvious answer is the entire court.

What should I do if an opposing player and I are involved in a long rally from baseline to baseline?

Try to break the pattern by using a dink or drop shot to pull your opponent in from his deep position. Or try a lob over the net man's head, hitting it so his partner has to play the shot with his backhand. If you are the steadier player, however, let him make the first mistake.

17.
STRATEGY

Do different surfaces call for different games?

Indeed they do, as all touring pros will testify.

Generally speaking, when you are confronted with a new surface you should concentrate more than usual on the ball, focusing on it from the time it leaves your opponent's racket and travels across the net until you make the contact.

Try to stay more on your toes, bouncing up and down as much as possible so that you are able to move quickly if the ball takes an unexpected bounce.

What are the basics of fast-court tactics?

HIT THE BALL ON THE RISE. When playing on a surface that is faster than what you are accustomed to, you must run quickly to the ball and hit it far out in front of your body as it rises from the bounce. All other things being equal, the player who attacks the most on a fast surface has the advantage. When you are playing from the baseline, think of hitting the ball so far in front of your body that your racket will follow through to the far service line.

GO TO THE NET WHENEVER POSSIBLE. Every time your opponent hits a short ball—one that bounces at the service line or closer to the net—hit your next shot deep. If you have hit a good approach shot you should be able to block the return at the net and win the point.

Jack Kramer, who was one of the best fast-court players, had a theory about playing on cement: if you hit forehands well enough and deep enough down the line and follow them to net, the percentages are in your favor.

CONCENTRATE ON WINNING YOUR SERVE. It is so difficult to break your opponent's serve on a fast court that you must concentrate on winning your own serve. Attempt to get your first serve in deep and well placed and then follow it to the net.

TRY TO BE STEADY ON RETURN OF SERVE. When your opponent is serving, watch the ball at all times, even at the point of contact. Don't take a big swing if he crunches it in. Hit your return as you would a volley, even though the ball has bounced. Try to block the ball back and keep it low.

DON'T OVERHIT. Just because the court is faster doesn't mean you have to hit harder. If you hit your shots normally, they will have more pace than on slow courts. Concentrate on hitting every shot with the center of your racket and then go in for the volley.

What are the basics of slow-court tactics?

SLIDE INTO THE BALL ON CLAY. On slow surfaces such as clay you must teach yourself to slide into the ball; otherwise you will overrun it. I still remember the first time I practiced on a European clay court at the Federation Cup matches in Turin, Italy, and had to admonish myself constantly, "Slide, you dummy. This isn't cement."

HIT THE BALL AT WAIST HEIGHT. This is so for almost every ground stroke but especially when playing on a slow court.

HIT MORE CROSS-COURT SHOTS. You must play angles

115

a lot more on a slow court in order to get your opponent off the court and set him up for a winner of your own. And because the surface is so slow, you have, in turn, a lot more time to cover the court yourself.

GET YOUR FIRST SERVE IN. This applies on any surface but especially on a slow court where your second serve will probably tend to hang in the air, giving your opponent the opportunity to make an offensive return.